Divine
COMPENSATION

DR. D. K. OLUKOYA

Divine Compensation

© 2014 DR. D. K. OLUKOYA

ISBN: 978- 978-920-111-2

Published July, 2014

Published by:
The Battle Cry Christian Ministries
322, Herbert Macaulay Street, Sabo, Yaba
P. O. Box 12272, Ikeja, Lagos.
www.battlecrystore.com
email: info@battlecrystore.com
       customercare@battlecrystore.com
       sales@battlecrystore.com
Phone: 0803-304-4239, 0816-122-9775

I salute my wonderful wife, Pastor Shade, for her invaluable support in the ministry.

I appreciate her unquantifiable support in the book ministry as the cover designer, art editor and art adviser.

All the Scriptures are from the King James Version

C O N T E N T S

CHAPTER 1

Divine
COMPENSATION

God is a God of compensation. God owes no man nothing. God is a God that gives rewards.

Ezekiel 29:17-22

> *And it came to pass in the seven and twentieth year, in the first month, in the first day of the month, the word of the LORD came unto me, saying, Son of man, Nebuchadrezzar king of Babylon caused his army to serve a great service against Tyrus: every head was made bald, and every shoulder was peeled: yet had he no wages, nor his army, for Tyrus, for the service that he had served against it: Therefore thus saith the Lord GOD; Behold, I will give the land of Egypt unto Nebuchadrezzar king of Babylon; and he shall take her multitude, and take her spoil, and take her prey; and it shall be the wages for his army. I have given him the land of Egypt for his labour*

wherewith he served against it, because they wrought for me, saith the Lord GOD. In that day will I cause the horn of the house of Israel to bud forth, and I will give thee the opening of the mouth in the midst of them; and they shall know that I am the LORD.

God energized Nebuchadnezzar to war against Tyre and he laid siege on it for 13 years. Unfortunately for him the long siege gave the people of Tyre the opportunity to smuggle out most of their stuff so by the time he took his place there was nothing there again. But he was on an assignment for the Almighty. The Lord said okay since you worked for me I must pay you back. Your compensation will be for you to take over the land of Egypt and everything that they have. God is a God of Divine compensation. I pray that where they have rejected you, you shall become the change in the name of Jesus.

God is a God of compensation. Don't ever think that anything you are doing for the Lord goes in vain. That's why it is a disaster when you come to the House of the Lord and you do nothing. You don't know what you are loosing. You are loosing the compensation plan of the Almighty.

GOD OF REWARD

People say their reward is in Heaven but there is also a reward now here on earth. God is a God of Divine compensation. For everything you do for Him you receive a reward. Those who are ready to go anywhere for Him, I pray that any power that wants to waste your labour shall be scattered in the name of Jesus.

1 Peter 5:10

> *But the God of all grace, who hath called us unto his eternal glory by Christ Jesus, after that ye have suffered a while, make you perfect, stablish, strengthen, settle you.*

The above passage prove to us that our famous song "Me I no go suffer, I no go beg for bread. Me I no go suffer, I no go beg for bread. God of miracle, na my papa O, God of miracle na my Papa O." Is a song of rebellion. The Bible did not promise us that we are not going to suffer at all. The Bible says "In this world ye shall have tribulations but be of good cheer I have overcome the world". He says "After that ye have suffered a while, He will make you perfect. He will establish, strengthen and then settle you. Declare this "O God arise and settle me by fire in the name of Jesus.

DIVINE SETTLEMENT

To settle is to appoint, to fix, to resolve something definitely and conclusively. To settle is to put you in your desired state, to give you rest. It is to make you stable and to get you establish. This is what it means to settle. Unbelievers may be using the language but it is a Bible language. I pray that the Lord God of Abraham, Isaac and Jacob shall settle you by fire in the name of Jesus. What you read about Nebuchadnezzar is a perfect example of Divine compensation. This is God rewarding an unbelieving nation for it's good service they had rendered to God. God is a faithful God and because of the faithfulness of God there is nothing that you do in the house of God that will go like that. There must be a reward. God often reward's some good works latter in order to make the reward better. I prophesy to your life that your season of Divine reward has come. Any good work or service you have done either for His kingdom or for mankind or far other people that you don't even know, you shall certainly and fully be compensated and the reward shall be for greater than your expectation. Every machinery that needs to be set in motion for you to receive you Divine compensation shall be set in motion now in the name of Jesus.

Nebuchadnezzar was not even born again but yet because he was God's instrument, he besieged the place for 13 years and he promised himself a good plunder, but he didn't get any so God had to reward him for his 13 years of hard labour. To encamp about a city for 13 years is not a joke but the Tylans were able to escape so God now compensated him by giving him Egypt. Today, the story of many Christians is like that of Nebuchadnezzar. They are working and they are not adequately compensated.

Satan is working behind the scene to rob them of the sweet of their sweat. Many have done many good works to mankind and for fellow human beings and for God but they are yet to receive the necessary payback. If God could be so concerned about Nebuchadnezzar, an unbeliever and He rewarded the man without the man even asking for it, how much more will He compensate His people who are serving Him with their heart. For many people, their blessings and compensation have already been given by Heaven but those things are being held by the forces of the enemy. I command the enemy holding your compensation to loose it's hold in the name of Jesus.

Esther 6:1-3

> *On that night could not the king*
> *sleep, and he commanded to bring*
> *the book of records of the chronicles;*

and they were read before the king. And it was found written, that Mordecai had told of Bigthana and Teresh, two of the king's chamberlains, the keepers of the door, who sought to lay hand on the king Ahasuerus. And the king said, What honor and dignity hath been done to Mordecai for this? Then said the king's servants that ministered unto him, There is nothing done for him.

Mordecai saved the life of the lazy king. He was recorded but not rewarded. Fortunately Haman the soul enemy of the Jews wanted to kill Mordecai and destroy the people of God. Unknown to him God was working behind the scene. The Haman that was planning to kill Mordecai and the Jeers was the one the king ordered to dress Mordecai in the robes of honor. I decree that God will humiliate your Haman and those who should remember you and they have forgotten you will loose their sleep until they remember you in the

SPIRITUAL WARFARE

God is a God of compensation. Mordecai was compensated later wonder to be compensated better. No good work will be lost. The reward will surely come. God does reward through work but the devil prevents so many people from being adequately rewarded. That's why every child of God needs to fight hard and go into spiritual warfare to deal with these forces.

What is Divine compensation? Divine compensation is for the Almighty to open your book of remembrance. Divine compensation is for the Almighty God to over answer your prayers. It is God rewarding you for your past labours of love. Divine compensation is Divine overpayment. Divine compensation is Divine pampering. Divine compensation is for the Almighty to make up for your past labours. It is for Heaven to reward you for all your activities. It is for the Almighty to redeem what Heaven owes you. Divine compensation is uncommon Heavenly reward, award and honour from Heaven. It is Divinely programmed honour to reward your labour. I prophecy to your life today that whether it is convenient for your enemy or not you will receive your divine compensation today in the name of Jesus.

GOD COMPENSATES

God is not a debtor to any man. He compensates.

Psalm 126:4

> *Turn again our captivity, O LORD, as the streams in the south.*

God compensates our tears with rejoicing. He turns our sorrow to joy. He says 'Whatever you sow in tears you shall reap in joy'. Meaning that the tears you are shedding in your prayers He will do the compensation and mesmerise your enemies and disgrace your Goliath.

Job 42:12

> *So the LORD blessed the latter end of Job more than his beginning: for he had fourteen thousand sheep, and six*

thousand camels, and a thousand yoke of oxen, and a thousand she asses.

God blessed the latter and of Job more than his beginning. God compensated Job for everything he had lost. You may be going through water and fire now. People may even be riding on your head now. They may be spitting at you now but God will soon usher you into a wealthy place in the name of Jesus.

Matthew 5:10-11

Blessed are they which are persecuted for righteousness' sake: for theirs is the kingdom of heaven. Blessed are ye, when men shall revile you, and persecute you, and shall say all manner of evil against you falsely, for my sake.

HEAVEN'S REWARD

God gives great reward for every suffering we suffer for Him. God compensated Joseph, Daniel,

David and many others for the humiliation they passed through. We need to believe the word of God.

Hebrew 6:10

> *For God is not unrighteous to forget your work and labour of love, which ye have shewed toward his name, in that ye have ministered to the saints, and do minister.*

God will not forget you no matter how things are presently for you. god will give you a voice where members of your family never got any voice in Jesus name. God will overrule the words of the enemy to promote you in the name of Jesus. I prophesy into you that where they say they do not want to see you, they shall see you in the name of Jesus.

When God puts you at the front nobody can pull you back. When God opens a door, nobody can shut it and when God shuts it nobody can open that door.

THE LOCATION

Every Divine compensation has a location. Where you are matters a lot. God is an expert at using the ridiculous to do the miraculous. You shall be in the right place at the right time in the name of Jesus. Your blessing has a geographical address. We serve a God of compensation. Moses started life in a rough way but God wanted to compensate him. Those who wanted to kill him were those who looked after him when he was a baby. God was feeding Moses by the hands of his own assassins. I pray that those who want to kill you shall protect you and those enemies that are pushing you shall only succeed in pushing you to your breakthrough in the name of Jesus.

The greater your destiny the harder your battle. I pray that every power arising to stop your star shall die in the name of Jesus. I pray that God will open your eyes to see your destiny location and the Lord will make the wrong people that are in your life to exit your life in the name of Jesus.

Your compensation day is tied to some helping people. I pray that your divine helpers shall locate you in the name of Jesus. Your compensation is tied to an appointed time. Every power objecting to your deliverance shall die in the name of Jesus.

PRAYER POINTS

1. Lord, give me divine prescription to my problems, in the name of Jesus.
2. I break all curses of leaking blessings, in the name of Jesus.
3. Let all spiritual holes in my life be closed with the blood of Jesus, in the name of Jesus.
4. Lord, help me to locate the defect in the clay of my life, in the name of Jesus.
5. Lord, let me be at the right place at the right time, in the name of Jesus.
6. I disarm every household enemy today, in the name of Jesus.
7. Let my enemies pitch their tents against one another, in the name of Jesus.
8. I frustrate and disappoint every instrument of the enemy fashioned against me, in the name of Jesus.
9. I seal my victory with the blood of Jesus.
10. I thank You Lord Jesus for answering my prayers.

▶ CHAPTER 2

Defeating
Anti-Breakthrough
Power

I would like you to read this message with rapt attention. However, before you go on, I would like you to pray these prayer points with all the seriousness that you can gather. By the time you would have finished reading this message, a divine exchange would have taken place in your life. The transformation that you will experience will make even your enemies to wonder. Not only that beloved, power and wealth will change hands in the Name of Jesus. This means that the powers that have been sitting on your breakthroughs, whether they are physical or spiritual, all of a sudden, those powers will somersault.

Also after reading this message there will be an over-turning and over taking. When the crisis starts, the purpose will be to bring you favor. Also long-term problems shall be disgraced. Many sisters who have lost their seat. will retrieve them. The servants that have been riding on the horse of the destiny of some people will fall down from that horse. If the doctors have qualified your situation as being 'hopeless', it shall experience the raw power of God today. Your labour of past years that the enemy has stolen, you shall repossess in the Name of Jesus. Many people collect blessings but they get filtered away. It is because they have evil baskets in their lives. If you are in that category the basket shall be melted away in the Name of Jesus. Do not allow this opportunity to pass you by.

PRAYERS!

1.   Any power that has tied me down die in the Name of Jesus.
2.   Every witchcraft power monitoring my breakthroughs die in the Name of Jesus.
3.   You 'Pharaoh' amongst my pursuers, you 'Goliath' amongst my oppressors, I bury you today in the Name of Jesus.

I want you to pull down the clouds of your breakthroughs today, by saying:

4.   O heavens, release my breakthroughs, in the Name of Jesus.

Psalm 124:7

> *"Our soul is escaped as a bird out of the snare of the fowlers: the snare is broken, and we are escaped".*

The first thing that I would like you to know is the fact that God is not a failure; therefore we His children should not be a failure in any way. God did not design anyone to come to this world and fail. Any failure we find in our lives is not the fault of God.

The verse above gives a wonderful picture of what is called breakthrough. Imagine the scene of a bird that has been caged. It has become limited even though it could travel for miles in the sky freely. It has been reduced to a creature that cannot move past 1foot upwards and downwards. Only God knows for how long it has been in the cage. Suddenly a particular power comes and breaks the cage open and the bird escapes. This is the picture of breakthrough.

BREAKTHROUGH SECRETS

It is a serious progress. It is possible for a person to progress but not in an appreciable way. If a person wants to go to Kaduna and sets out on foot, he would be moving, which means he or she is making progress but it is a slow one. Breakthrough is serious progress, advancement. I know that you want advancement; otherwise you would not have picked this message up to read. Those who know that there is a better level and want to get there are the ones that read messages like this. I know that the Lord will touch you through it and you will become a completely changed person in the Name of Jesus.

Breakthrough is a positive boost. You could be doing well and you start doing better. It is a forward development, an important discovery. You could have been on one spot for years and you do not know what is going wrong. All of a sudden, God opens your eyes to see what it is. A person could have been eating form the table of darkness for a long time. Then one day, God opens his eyes to see what is going wrong.

In one of our branches, we preached a message on the strongman. There was a woman at the service, who had just lost her husband. she prayed vigorously and her blouse was soaked in sweat. When she got home, her house-help welcomed her and congratulated her for having started to pray. The woman wondered and the girl said she was the one that killed her husband. The woman said she had to leave the house. The girl said she would leave but that the woman should know that she had initiated her children into witchcraft. For fifteen years, this woman did not know that her enemy was in her pocket. There are many people like that whose eyes need to be opened. You should know who the rat in your business is, and who the aggressor in your camp is; and who the unfriendly friends are.

BREAKTHROUGH POINTS

Breakthrough is breaking through a barrier, which the Psalmist calls "Jumping over a wall." It is when you penetrate your enemy's defence. They have been trying to defend you but all of a sudden, you move in. it is an anointed increase, which will make people wonder what is happening to you, it is being lifted above all the enemies round about you. It is promotion, enrichment, betterment. It is a positive headway.

Sometime ago we prayed for a young man. He had A's in all the subjects he sat for the school certificate examination. However, whenever he sat for the joint matriculation examination his result was withheld because his score was always too high and it was assumed that he cheated. One day he attended an MFM prayer meeting and we prayed for him. That night he had a dream where he saw himself at the gate of a university in the south and a masquerade was standing there, saying that he would not go in he got to another university in the north and the masquerade was at the gate and it said he would not go in. He saw himself in front of another university which he had never been to before and he still saw the masquerade which did not allow him to enter. For the first time in his life it became clear to him, that there was an enemy attached to his breakthrough. I pray that any power assigned to your breakthrough shall be destroyed today in the Name of Jesus.

A RADICAL EXPANSION

Breakthrough is a radical expansion; an exceptional maximisation; an enlargement, a turning point. It is when you are going the way of poverty and all of a sudden, there is a turning point. It is when you are going the way of frustration and all of a sudden, there is a turn around. It is when the doctor's diagnosis spells doom and you do not know that doctors do not have the last say; all of a sudden, there is a turn around for the best and the doctors are now surprised.

A woman came for prayers some years ago; she was 48 years old and had no child. After the prayers, she got pregnant. The scan showed that she had fibroid and that she should get it removed. She said she wouldn't go through any operation. She sought a second opinion from another doctor and the scan showed fibroid. She said she would not undergo the operation but would tell her pastor. She told me and we started to pray. I asked her to go back for another scan and she went to another doctor.

There, it was discovered that she really had fibroids but she also had a baby in the womb, which the first two doctors did not see. It means that they would have killed the baby in an attempt to remove the fibroid. I pray that any power that wants to destroy good things in your life, shall be destroyed in the Name of Jesus.

Beloved, you and I have been called to a battle; whether you like it or not you are in the battlefront. Whether you believe it or not war has been declared against you. If you say that you have never offended anyone to warrant hostility against you, then I would ask you if Jesus offended anybody to warrant the treatment that He received form the Jews.

The devil does not let go easily on his prey; he has to be forced. The enemy of our soul will not give you honorary victory at all. Many people have honorary degrees; this means that they did not sweat to study for it. They were given free of charge. The enemy will not give you that kind of freedom that you did not sweat for. If there is any problem in your life now, the truth is that your life has something worth contesting for. That is all. You might wonder why you have problems; do you realize that if you do not it means you are finished. If the enemy sees that you are useless and without consequence to his kingdom, he will leave you alone and not bother you at all because you are not a threat to his kingdom.

ANTI-BREAKTHROUGH POWERS

They are powers that are saying 'NO' to your breakthroughs. They are the ones that hinder you form moving forward. They are the powers that make people to doubt God's intervention in their situation. They are powers that have formed a covenant to resist you.

THE BREAKTHROUGH

A woman had five sons. They got married and for many years none of them had a child. The fifth one was given a book from MFM. He did not understand the prayers but he prayed them anyway. One day the Lord spoke to him that he should not sleep with his wife for the first seven days of their wedding. He told his fiancee and she agreed. On the wedding night the bride came close and he reminded her of their agreement. The following day the same thing happened. On the third day the newly wedded wife got angry and struggled with her husband and even tore his clothes. He stood firm and did not sleep with her. On the forth day, he got a phone call from home that his mother was dying.

The couple rushed there and the mother said she had a confession to make. She said she was a witch and had donated the sperms of the five sons and that was why they had no children. The covenant she made was to spiritually collect the sperms of her sons on the first three days of their marriage. She had succeeded in the lives of the other four. When it got to the turn of the last one, she found out that they were not having sexual intercourse. She had only three days to carry out the operation; that was why the pressure was high from the bride on the third day.

-28-

Since the mother could not donate the sperm, she had to die. That was why she sent for the man and his wife and then she died. That brother is the only one that has children out of the five men today.

Take this prayer point with holy anger beloved:

1.   Every internal power assigned against my breakthroughs, die in the Name of Jesus. How did that woman transport herself into their bedroom without their knowledge? She did not go there physically. It means there are many things moving about that our physical eyes cannot see.

Take these prayer points:

1.   Every power flying against my breakthroughs die in the Name of Jesus.

2.   Let there be a release of the anointing that breaks yokes upon my life in the Name of Jesus.

ANTI-BREAKTHROUGH POWERS

Anti-breakthrough powers are powers contending for a person's victory. They are powers that are designated to stagnate a person. They limit and stagnate progress. A man was experiencing stagnation in every way and every thing. One day, a friend sent him a forged foreign passport, with his photograph on it, to travel to that country. When he arrived that country, he passed the customs and immigration counters as an indigene. Suddenly one of the officers called him back and asked if the passport was his and he said yes. The officer asked him to mention the names of three popular supermarkets in that country but he could not. He was asked to mention the names of three daily newspapers and he could not. He was shown a coin and asked to say how much it was but he could not. It then became clear beyond any reasonable doubt that he had forged the passport. He was deported immediately. His life had been limited by the powers that stagnate. Anti-breakthrough powers are always sad and unhappy when a person starts making progress. They are bent on returning or retaining a person in poverty.

They are powers of the night that spiritually steal from people. They circulate the names of people for evil.

I used to tell a friend to be fervent in prayer, but he would laugh at me. He studied abroad so he did not believe that there are evil powers anywhere. One day, as he was reviewing the videotape that his monitoring camera recorded in his office, he was shocked. He saw his secretary with a live cock; she killed it and smeared underneath his chair with the blood. He ran to me with the tape, crying that he had sat on the chair. Soon afterwards, he lost a huge, multi-million Naira contract that was almost his. I reminded him of the fact that he needed prayers. He has now become a prayer warrior.

Anti-breakthrough powers nullify favour. They are the ones that set up girl and boy friends from the pit of hell, in order to make people commit immoral acts with them and sin against God, thus, losing their breakthroughs. They are the powers that rage when a person's breakthrough is close-by. They are the powers that cause chaos when a person is about to shine. They are inherited powers that have been assigned to destroy.

Today is the day that you will pray some serious prayers. They could sound strange but they are arrows of prayers that will fly far and wide unhindered.

THE WAY OUT

What to do

1. **Realize that any sin in your life will hinder breakthroughs.** Sin could be as simple as anger, bitterness, envy, drunkenness, fornication, etc.
2. **Know that the power of God is above all powers.**
3. **Wage war against anti-breakthrough powers.**

There was a family of five girls. They all got married and one by one, they had problems with their husbands and they returned to their family house, where their parents and grandmother lived. One day, the youngest of them came across our book titled: Pray Your Way To Breakthroughs. She prayed all the prayers in it fervently that night from midnight till 1.00a.m. The following morning, their grandmother came to see her, to ask her which kind of prayers she was praying the previous night. She advised her to stop praying them and continue praying the ones they pray in their church. The ones she recommended are the prayers that recount stories and describe themselves without fire in them.

PRAYER BOMBARDMENT

The trouble is that those prayers worked in the 1930s, but now, the enemy has changed gears and is now on the fast lane. When the sister heard this she knew that there was trouble. She then decided to start form page 1 of the book. She prayed from midnight till 3.00a.m. The following morning the grandmother came and warned her that those prayers were dangerous and that the sister was planning to kill someone with them. The sister apologized but she knew that she would not stop.

The third night, she started from page one and prayed even the prayers that did not sound relevant to her situation she prayed till 6.00a.m. By the time everybody woke up, they found their grandmother dead on her bed. As they were looking through her belongings, a padlock was found. The sister broke it open and in it was a list with the names of the five sisters written on it. There was also a cotton wool with bloodstain on it. That meant that as far as they were menstruating, they would not stay in their husband's house. The youngest poured anointing oil on the padlock, list and cotton wool, then burnt it with petrol. That evening, the husband of the first-born came begging that his wife should come back home. By the end of that week, all five ladies were back in their husband's houses.

Beloved, we have arrived at an arena where you cannot afford to joke with the enemy or have pity on him. We have arrived the arena where every problem has to bend or bow; your enemy has made a mistake today. Take these prayers with holy aggression:

1. Every power assigned against my breakthroughs, your time is up, therefore die in the Name of Jesus.
2. Every house of shame constructed against me, scatter in the Name of Jesus.
3. Every power dragging my progress in the ground, your time is up die in the Name of Jesus.

Sometimes people feel movements in their bodies; those are anti-breakthrough serpents. They block roads of progress. Today if you are in that category, you will receive the touch of the power of God. The Lord will give you your own letter of breakthrough today in the Name of Jesus. Right now visualize those things that you do not want in your life anymore. Name them one by one and pray like this:

My Father, I come before You today, I know that You care for me and you will not allow me to be messed up by the enemy. It is written that You have given me power to tread upon serpents and scorpions and over every power of the enemy, and nothing shall by any means hurt me. Right now, every serpent and scorpion assigned against me is dead in the Name of Jesus. As from today, every power of Egypt that I saw before, I shall see them no more in the Name of Jesus.

Pray these prayers with holy aggression:

1. I dissolve every anti-breakthrough strategy, in Jesus' name
2. Let the hands of evil refuse to perform their enterprise in any area of my life, in the name of Jesus.
3. I decree that there shall not be compromise and dialogue between me and my enemies, in the name of Jesus.
4. I pull down all strongholds of evil over my life and the lives of any members of my family, in the name of Jesus.
5. Lord, close the gap between where I am and where You want me to be.
6. Let all demonic jailers be roasted, in the name of Jesus.

Beloved, before we go into the message, let us start by uttering a miracle cry. Pray aggressively like this: "Oh Lord, convert my disappointment into miracle, in the name of Jesus."

We will start by looking at some verses on miracle cry in the Bible.

Psalm 56:9 says,

> "When I cry unto thee, then shall my enemies turn back. This I know, for God is for me."

Psalm 61: I - 2 says,

> "Hear my cry, O God: attend to my prayer. From the end of the earth will I cry unto thee, when my heart is overwhelmed: lead me to the rock that is higher than I."

Psalm 107:26-27 says,

> "They mount up to the heaven, they go down again to the depths: their soul is melted because of trouble.

CHAPTER 3

The
Miracle
Cry

They reel to and fro, and stagger like a drunken man, and are at their wit's end." (That is, they have done everything they can, doctors have done their best and everybody has said, "Finish, this is the limit which we can help you," then what did they do.)

Verses 28-31 say,

> *"Then they cry unto the Lord in their trouble, and He bringeth them out of their distresses. He maketh the storm a calm, so that the waves thereof are still. Then are they glad because they be quiet; so He bringeth them unto their desired haven. Oh that men would praise the Lord for His goodness and for His wonderful works to the children of men!"*

THE CRY

You can say well, these are Bible theories, but there was a man who practicalised it. Mark 10:46 says, *"And they came to Jericho: and as He went out of Jericho with his disciples and a great number of people, blind Bartimaeus, the son of Timaeus, sat by the highway side begging. And when he heard that it was Jesus of Nazareth, he began to cry out, and say, Jesus thou son of David, have mercy on me."* That was his cry.

Jesus was going out of Jericho on His last journey to Jerusalem and blind Bartimaeus was sitting there begging. When he heard that it was Jesus, he cried out, "Jesus thou son of David, have mercy on me."

Verse 48 says,

> *"And many charged him that he should hold his peace. (Shut up, die in your blindness) but he cried the more a great deal, (Meaning that he increased the volume) Thou son of David, have mercy on me."*

So he was asked to keep quiet, but he refused to be silent.

In verse 49, the cry did something to Jesus, *"And Jesus stood still, (He could not go further because it is not possible for the Lord to neglect a deep cry) and commanded him to be called. And they called the blind man (the same people who said shut up) saying unto him, Be of good comfort, rise He calleth thee."*

Verse 50:

> *"And he casting away his garment, rose and came to Jesus."*

When he was told to keep quiet, he refused and Jesus sent for him. He cast away his garment that was disturbing him, so that his movement would be fast.

Verse 51 says, "And Jesus answered and said unto him, What will thou that I should do unto thee? (a very interesting question, just as He is asking you as you are reading this message now.) The blind man said unto him, Lord, that I might receive my sight." Why did Jesus ask him that kind of question? Jesus asked him that question because his first prayer point was mercy, and as far as the Bible is concerned, there are different kinds of mercy in it. So Jesus wanted him to identify the one he wanted.

There was a crusade somewhere and the Lord was doing quite a lot of wonders there. But everyday, there was this blind man by the door begging alms. One day, a brother after coming from evangelism was annoyed and said to him, "Mr. man, there is miracle happening there and you are sitting down here begging. In holy anger the brother laid hands on him and said, "Receive your sight, in the name of Jesus," His eyes opened and he could see. People who saw it jumped up and were rejoicing. But to their amazement, the man who was formerly blind was crying. He said, "Do you see what you have done now, where will I get the kind of   m o n e y

So it was important for Jesus to ask blind Bartimaeus what he wanted. And Jesus used to ask this kind of question a lot. Look at the man he found by the pool of Bethesda, He looked at the man and asked him, "Wilt thou be made whole?" May be all that blind man wanted was ten kobo. The man was busy telling stories: "There is nobody to put me inside the water, etc," instead of the man saying what he wanted. Jesus asked many questions in the Bible. I counsel you to find time and study them. It is a very good Bible study.

SPIRITUAL BLINDNESS

If you are a good reader of the Bible, you will find out that the Bible uses blindness a lot as a figure of ignorance and darkness. So when it talks about the Messiah as the light of the world to open the blind eyes, it is talking about the darkness that the enemy has constructed in the lives of people. This darkness is being taken away by Jesus Christ who is the light of the world and the Son of God. When the Bible says, "In whom the god of this world has blinded the minds of those that believe not;" it is talking about another kind of blindness.

Those with blind hearts find it very hard to understand the gospel no matter how much you preach. Jesus called the Pharisees, "Thou blind Pharisees," not because their eyes were blind, but because they were spiritually blind. It is only the light of Christ that can remove ignorance and spiritual darkness. He says, "I am the light of the world, he that followeth me shall not walk in darkness but shall have the light of life."

When you see a Bible story or parable, don't just look at it like that on the surface. God uses them to teach deep lessons. Blindness and darkness are serious problems. The effect of blindness is very bad. A spiritually blindman will not see where he is going in the spirit. He will be stumbling over unseen objects in the spirit. Such a person can go to the enemy's camp to receive help because he cannot see beyond his nose. He will be warming himself in the fire of the enemy and he will be getting in the ways of others and obstructing them. When you are spiritually blind, you will be confused and even spoil things for other people around you.

For example, a blind father will bring charms home and distribute them to his children who are ignorant. A blindman will miss all the beauty of light and beautiful things that God has made around him. So spiritual blindness is worse than physical blindness. I want you to pray the prayer of the Psalmist which says, "Open thou my eyes that I might behold wondrous things." Was the Psalmist blind? No. He was talking about the eyes of the spirit man. I like you to lay your hands on your chest and pray this one aggressively: "Every spiritual darkness, fly away from my heart, in the name of Jesus.

What are the other lessons we can pick from the miracle cry of Blind Bartimaeus?

1.   **Do not waste time:** Ask for the touch of the Lord while He is still around. That popular song says, "...While on others thou art calling, do not pass me by." Jesus never passed that way again. He was on His way to die. Bartimaeus had his last opportunity and made very good use of it.

Many people hear the gospel not knowing that they could be hearing it for the last time. Perhaps, if they had listened, they could have been saved.

WIGGLESWORTH'S EXAMPLE

Brother Wigglesworth who was an aggressive evangelist said that one day, God said to him, "Stand up son, and go into the market place. I have eleven souls to save through you today." He went to the market place and stayed there. As people were passing by, he kept asking the Lord, "Is it this one Lord?" If the Lord said no, he would let the person go. But when the Lord said, "Yes that is the one," Wigglesworth in his known crude manner, would rush to the person and say, "Are you born again?" If his answer was no, he would say to him, "You must get born again now." And right there in the market place, he would open the Bible and begin to teach the person. Generally, all the people he approached that way gave their lives to Christ.

There was a day the Lord told him that eleven people would give their lives through him in the market place on that day. He got ten, and the eleventh person was not forthcoming before the market started closing and he too was getting impatient. He stood there until everybody went away from the market. Suddenly somebody came along on a chariot and the Lord said, "That is the man." Wigglesworth ran and jumped on the chariot. He said to the man, "It is because of you I have been waiting for so long, give your life now," and the man said, "Yes sir," and gave his life. Two days later, Wigglesworth saw in the newspaper that the man died the next day. This is why spiritual opportunities are to be used to the fullest.

I do not believe that you are reading this bulletin by chance, so the opportunity God has given to you to read this message must be used to the fullest. Jesus never passed that way again.

2.   **Learn to cry out: Bartimaeus cried for mercy.** He understood the act of begging very

well and he applied it. If men will take the place of blind beggars before God and call for mercy, they will find it. Romans 10:13 says, *"For whosoever shall call upon the name of the Lord shall be saved."* Sometimes, all we need to do is to cry for God's mercy. His power is able to deliver. I like you to close your eyes again and pray like this: "Lord have mercy upon me, in the name of Jesus."

3. **Have faith:** The man had never seen Jesus before because he was blind but by faith he believed and cried unto him. It was first a cry and later, he saw. The world's order of doing things is seeing before believing, but heaven's order is believing before seeing. When Martha said to Jesus, "If you had been here, my brother would not have died." Jesus answered her with a straight single sentence, "Thy brother shall live again." She said, "Yes I know, he would rise again on the resurrection morning." And Jesus said, "I am the resurrection. Said I not

unto thee that if thou wouldest believe, thou shouldest see the glory of God." Very simple, if you don't believe, the glory of God will be far away from you.

4. **Do not let others kill your faith:** Many people asked blind Bartimaeus to keep quiet, but he did not listen to them. The person who is saying, "A whole you," can not lift one finger to help you out of your problem. There was one boy that used to come to Mountain of Fire and Miracles ministries and his parents did not quite like it. They tried to stop him but could not, so they tried using charms. After putting some charms in their mouths, they woke the boy up at 12 midnight and said, "Hear now, you will not go to that place again. Do you hear, as from today, the memory of that place will be removed from your brain, you will not go there again." While they went away rejoicing, the boy was laughing at their foolishness on his bed. The next day, he was the first to arrive here.

Millions of people are kept from heaven by the thought of what others will say. Sometimes, when an altar call is made, some people will open their eyes and first of all look around their surrounding to see whether there is anybody with his hand up before they raise theirs, and when they cannot find any, they keep their hands down. This is how many people perish. Some people come to crusades with their girlfriends and boyfriends and when the word of God hits them where they are, they will not be able to come out because of their partners. Let it be clear to you that whether you do good or bad, people will talk. Jesus said, "Woe unto you when they say that you are good." It means that you are one of them. But immediately you begin to live the kind of life God wants you to live, you will be criticized and attacked. If you are going to be listening to what people are saying or thinking about you before you serve the Lord, you will end up in trouble.

Millions of people are kept away from their breakthroughs by listening to what others will say. God will hold you responsible if you allow your life to be directed by men. Bartimaeus refused to be influenced by those around him. He told them, "It is easy for you to be saying keep quiet, but I am the one that is blind." He screamed and Jesus stopped.

5.   **Perseverance:** The Lord has a method of sometimes waiting for sometime before He answers. Not because He does not know that there is problem, but He likes to test the reality of your desire. When you refuse to be discouraged, that is the mark of true faith. Some people fall under pressure. A man had problems. One night, he felt so sad that he went to bed discouraged. As he slept, he had a dream in which he found himself in a market place. At the market place, he stumbled into a particular stall, with Mr. devil written on it and the devil was there too. The man said, "Mr devil, so you too are selling things in this market? The devil said, "Yes." Then, he began to look at what he was selling and saw items like hypertension, bad luck, cancer, all kinds of

terrible things. He looked through and said to the devil, "Hello sir, what is the most expensive thing in your stall? And he pointed at "discouragement," and told the man that when he wants to catch Christians, he uses it. So when they get discouraged, their faith goes down and they will not be able to pray and then fear will move in. And when that happens, worry will follow it, and then, he the devil will move in. Discouragement is a powerful weapon of the enemy.

6.   **Violent faith:** Another thing you can learn from this miracle cry of Bathimeaus is the principle of violent faith. Jesus said to him, thy faith has made you whole. Jesus healed him because he believed and asked. God honours faith. It is the appointed medium through which blessings come to us.

7.   **The holy haste of Bartimaeus:** When Jesus told him to come, he moved like thunder, threw away his garment so that it would not hinder him and came to Jesus.

Remember, in countries that are cold, beggars used to have lots of heavy clothing. So he had lots of things to discard. He pulled them off and started to move and then his eyes got opened immediately and he started seeing. You too can call upon Him before He passes by. And now He is calling all men to repentance.

I will like you to utter twenty-one miracle cries that can fetch you twenty-one miracles after reading this message. But before you do that, let us look at some enemies of miracle cries.

1.   **Lack of Repentance:** Sin is an enemy of holy cry. Any willful sinner is going to hell fire no matter what they call him or her.

2.   **Unbelief:** You must cast the garment of unbelief away so that it does not hinder you.

3.   **Hatred:** If you hate anybody, the Bible says, you are a murderer. There was war in a city. The enemies were pursuing two men. These two people were arch enemies, they did not like each other at all. One of them ran and hid himself inside a pit. The other

one ran into the bush and hid himself there. The enemies were searching for them and after some time, they got the man in the pit and wanted to kill him, and he was begging them saying, "Please sirs, my wife just delivered a baby five days ago, please have mercy, don't render my baby fatherless. But the other man hiding in the bush shouted and told them that his enemy was lying and in the process, he exposed himself and the people looking for both of them were able to kill them. That is what hatred does. Believers should not hate anybody, the only person they should hate is the devil.

4. **Unforgiving spirit:** If you refuse to forgive those who offend you, you will be looking for tormentors. You must forgive all who have offended you.

5. **Ingratitude:** If you are not grateful for what God has done for you, if you do not count your blessings, you are inviting trouble into your life.

You must utter these miracle cries aggressively. Determine that your situation must change today. God does not mind going to the uttermost part of the earth to root out your blessings. God does not even mind removing a whole town because of one person.

A man shared a testimony with me. He led a prayer meeting somewhere and called a fire prayer point which says, "All those who are planning evil against me, gather here now in the name of Jesus. Everybody prayed and the spirits started coming. When they came. He told the congregation, "Now, issue the fire of judgement upon them," and they began to call on the fire of judgement. The man said he prayed like a mad person until his clothes were soaked. A week after that time, he started to get information from his village. The first person to die was their chief priest before others followed. Many of us do not know those who are in charge of our cases but when you fire a divine arrow, anything can happen.

MIRACLE CRIES

1. I break every hold of witchcraft over my life, in the name of Jesus.

2. All my unfavorable situations, change now, in the name of Jesus.

3. I command all my battles to be converted to blessings, in the name of Jesus.

4. You mountain confronting me, crumble now, in the name of Jesus.

5. I bind every desert spirit, in the name of Jesus.

6. Oh Lord, beer me up on the wings of the eagle before my enemies, in the name of Jesus.

7. Lay your hands on your eyes and pray like this :O Lord, anoint my eyes to see my divine opportunities, in the name of Jesus. As you are laying your hands on your eyes, where you never thought good things could come, I pray, that the Lord will begin to open your eyes to see them. I also pray that

unfriendly friends shall now be revealed unto you. I pray that every unrepentant witch, working against you, shall confess and die before you, in the name of Jesus.

8.   I refuse to allow my past to disturb my future, in the name of Jesus.

9.   I bind the strong man of financial problems, in the name of Jesus.

10.   Let every satanic battle confronting me, fall apart now, in the name of Jesus.

11.   Every crooked and difficult area of my life, straighten out now, in the name of Jesus.

12.   Let the spirit of excellence manifest in every area of my life, in the name of Jesus.

13.   Let the fear of me fill the mind of my enemy, in the name of Jesus.

14.   Let divine harvest meet harvest in my life, in the name of Jesus

15.   I receive power to leap over every wall that the enemy has built against me, in Jesus' name. 16. Let the mockery of my enemy result into my advancement, in the name of Jesus.

17. Oh Lord, turn my mourning into dancing and my tears to joy, in the name of Jesus.

18. Oh Lord, display your power against every unrepentant opposition, in the name of Jesus.

19. Oh Lord, convert my opposition to promotion, in the name of Jesus.

20. Let every Goliath defying my prayers. be paralyzed, in the name of Jesus.

21. I laugh my enemies to scorn, in the name of Jesus.

CHAPTER 4

The
God
Of
Daniel

Beloved, I want you to understand this very well the God of Daniel is the God of revelation. I came from a very poor family; so poor that, daddy would complain that the soup mummy prepared was not good enough, forgetting that it was the amount of money he gave her, that determined the ingredients she bought. It was that bad; so when I got born again I began to pray and God began to show me certain things and I made up my mind that I will not be poor. You must know where you are coming from so that you can work hard to get to where you are going. Many people who are supposed to be discreet in what they do are loud, thus the enemy finds his way into their life. Maybe nobody knows them on the street before, but the day they throw a party and lavish money on people, those who did not know them would know that they have money to flaunt. I knew where I was coming from and so I was able to pray and work hard. Later I got a scholarship to travel abroad. The ticket, school fees, everything was given to me. I knew that if I made noise about it, I would probably not go. I kept silent and prepared. It was on the day I was travelling that people saw me in my suits, with my suitcase. Sometimes we need to be discrete so as not to expose our secrets to the enemy.

During my stay in England, I worked hard and one day my supervisor advised that I should take a break and go to Nigeria on holiday. He persistently told me to take a break. One night, I had a dream, where I saw myself at the Ikeja Airport. Our flight to London was announced and I looked round but could not find the exit to the tarmac. Eventually I found it, but by the time I got to the tarmac, the aeroplane had taken off and I was left behind. That dream made me to know, that I should not go home. So I told my supervisor that I would not go. Some Nigerian students went and during their stay in Nigeria, there was a 'Coup d' Etat'. All borders and airports were closed and no one could travel out. By the time they got back, some of them had missed examinations, some failed woefully. Some could not go back to England because their sponsors were killed in the 'Coup d' Etat' and that marked the end of their career. I could have fallen into that category too.

You need divine visions to sort out your life.

The God of Daniel is the God of sovereign power.

Daniel 2:21:

> *"And He changeth the times and the seasons: He removeth kings, and setteth up kings: He giveth wisdom unto the wise and knowledge to them that know understanding".*

He is the God who rules nations; He has the power to remove a king and replace him with another one. He has the power to crush the pride of earthly rulers. He does not mind giving the sack to anyone whose position is hindering the progress of His children. Today, the strongman that constitutes a hindrance to your breakthrough shall be bound and your breakthroughs shall be released in the Name of Jesus.

I met a young Nigerian in England. I preached to him and he always made fun of me. He was a First Class Material. He cleared his Masters Degree with a distinction and he got ready to leave. We all bade him goodbye. After a few days, I received a letter which had the logo of the maximum prison on the envelope. I read it and found out that it was that young man. He asked me to come to the prison to pay him a visit. He asked me to buy a few things and bring for him. He said he realized that what I was telling him was the truth. I made up my mind that I would not go for fear of being arrested as an accomplice. I put the letter somewhere and the Lord talked to me expressly, that I should go to the prison to see the young man.

When I got there, he burst into tears, lamenting that if he had listened to me, he would not have been in prison. He said he got born again there and had been preaching to the inmates about Jesus, that they only made fun of him. I prayed with him, he confessed his sins to the Lord and we asked God to intervene in his situation. When I got back to town, I informed other brethren and we started to pray. On the day he was taken to court, we were in the court room, praying silently in tongues.

The judge was very aggressive he promised to deal ruthlessly with him. We had to call on the God of Daniel; we asked for a replacement of the judge, with a more lenient person. At the next hearing, it was another judge that presided over the case. The new judge looked at the brother and asked if it was true that he bagged a First Class Honours Degree in Nigeria, and that he got a Distinction in Masters Degree in England. The brother answered in the affirmative. The Judge then said, for an intelligent person to steal money, he had to be mad; therefore, he would not jail him in England, but repatriate him to Nigeria. We knew that the brother was not mad; we knew that the God of Daniel was at work.

The God of Daniel is the God of secrets.

Daniel 2:22:

> *"He revealeth the deep and secret things: He knoweth what is in the darkness, and the light dwelleth with Him".*

He is the God that reveals secrets. All the secrets of the universe are known to God. All the past, present and future are known to God. He can tell the destinies of nations. He can tell you what will happen in the next five or six years. If there is any conspiracy against you, God can show you the secret. God can make you discover a witchcraft meeting and you will hear their discussions so that you can counter their plans.

As you are there right now there is a secret about your life that you would need to know. Immediately you know it, your life will explode. Find out what it is.

Many years ago, we preached a message about destiny and prosperity. A woman was there and when she got home, she prayed fervently. She was learned, had a job, but was very poor. The Lord drew her attention to the piece of land behind her house, and told her in a clear voice, to start planting vegetables there. She thought it was the devil that was making a denigrating proposal to her. She bound the voice in anger because she had a

Master's Degree in Education. The Lord made her to know that He was the One speaking and she complied. She started the vegetable farm and it was as if the whole town was waiting for her. They abandoned every other vegetable and bought hers. It got to an embarrassing stage where nobody else could sell vegetables until hers, were finished. Within one year, this teacher that used to be poor, had enough money to build a house with proceeds from vegetable- farming. I pray that the Lord will reveal to you the secrets that will move your life forward.

The God of Daniel is the God of deliverance.

Daniel 6:20-22:

"And when he came to the den, he cried with a lamentable voice unto Daniel: and the king spake and said to Daniel: "O Daniel, servant of the living God, is thy God, whom thou servant continually, able to deliver thee from the lions?" Then said Daniel unto the king: "O king, live

for ever. My God hath sent his angel, and hath shut the lions' mouths, that they have not hurt me: forasmuch as before Him innocence was found in me; and also before thee, O king, have I done no hurt".

Immediately Daniel got into the Lion's den, the lions recognized him as the son of the Lion of the Tribe of Judah. Lions do not eat lions. So they did not touch him.

One day, a friend's wife was traveling in a Luxurious bus. Suddenly, one of the passengers asked the driver to stop for him to ease himself. The driver stopped and someone came to the woman to say that a man at the back wanted to see her that he was her husband's classmate at school. The woman got up to go and see the person. A few seconds later, a trailer ran into the Luxurious bus and all the people sitting at the front where the woman got up from perished. The amazing part of the story is the fact that the woman could not see the person who came to call her to the back.

That must have been God's angel of deliverance that came to call her out of danger.

The God of Daniel is the God of signs and wonders.

Daniel 6:26-27:

"I make a decree, that in every dominion of my kingdom men tremble and fear before the God of Daniel: for he is the living God, and steadfast for ever, and His kingdom that which shall not be destroyed, and His dominion shall be even unto the end. He delivereth and rescueth, and He worketh signs and wonders in heaven and in earth, who hath delivered Daniel from the power of the lions"

Luke 21:15:

"For I will give you a mouth and wisdom, which all your adversaries shall not be able to gainsay nor resist".

Daniel 1:8-9:

> *"But Daniel purposed in his heart that he would not defile himself with the portion of the king's meat, nor with the wine which he drank: therefore he requested of the prince of the eunuchs that he might not defile himself. Now God had brought Daniel into favour and tender love with the prince of the eunuchs".*

There was a supernatural ability that allowed Daniel to have knowledge, skill and wisdom. Knowledge, skill and wisdom are the things that you need, to help you get to the top. The kind that your friends and enemies cannot contend or compare with. I pray that that will be your lot in the Name of Jesus.

In 1998, we had a programme dedicated to teachers. It was a deliverance programme organised to address the poverty of teachers. We prayed the prayers for knowledge, skill and wisdom on that day. A teacher came with her son who was a pilot. She had seven children who still depended on her.

This woman had all the problems in the world. She could not 'make ends meet' at the end of the month and had to borrow money from her subordinates, even though she was the Vice Principal of her school. Her children were grown and were university graduates, but depended on her. One of them was a pilot and was working with a local airline but it was as if he was not working at all. During the deliverance programme they both prayed fervently on that day.

After a while there was an advertisement in the Newspapers, that an American airline was recruiting pilots. The young man applied and he was invited to an interview. His performance impressed the airline and he was recruited immediately. When he heard the good news, he fainted. He was given a ten-year contract worth millions of dollars and was given thousands of Dollars to pay off the company he was working with. This job changed his life and that of the

DR. D. K. OLUKOYA

members of his family. His mother came to show me the keys to the jeep he bought for her and narrated how 'power changed hands' in their lives. He bought her a house and all she needed, and he went to the U.S.A. to assume his post as pilot.

That is what happens when there is a supernatural knowledge and skill imparted into your life. The God of Daniel is still the same today. If you want Him to bestow upon you, the anointing for skill, wisdom and knowledge, He is ready to do it. The God of Daniel is the One you will find in Daniel 1:17. He reveals the truth to His children through dreams and revelations.

The God of Daniel is the God of Divine Revelation.

Daniel 1:17:

> "As for these four children, God gave them knowledge and skill in all learning and wisdom: and Daniel had understanding in all visions and dreams".

He can reveal to you before an interview all the questions that you will be asked and you will know all the secrets before you get there. Since the beginning of the history of the world, there has never been a man or woman, who had the ability to have divine dreams who ever failed, but the problem is this; instead of having divine dreams these days, Christians are seeing themselves being pursued by masquerades in their dreams. They are being harassed by spirit husbands or wives and all sorts of terrible dreams. The God of Daniel is the One Who is able to set aside all these terrible dreams and replace them with night visions and revelations.

A sister got married and on the wedding night, she refused the traditional 'pouring of water' on her feet. The groom's mother got angry and promised to show her 'pepper'. That night, the bride had a dream, where she saw her mother-in-law dip her hand into her stomach and pulled out her womb. She went to the back of their house and nailed the womb to the wall. Although this sister was born again, she did not know anything about spiritual warfare. She remembered having the dream but did not know that it could have any implication on her. She discovered that she could not get pregnant, even though medical tests and scans could not detect anything wrong with her. She was childless for 16 years. The Lord brought her to MFM and she started to pray fire prayers. One night, she had a dream, where she saw her mother-in-law come into the house with her womb and she collected it. In real life the mother-in-law died many years before then. That was how the sister got her breakthrough. She got pregnant and now has children.

I know that the God of Daniel shall visit you today. However, if you are reading this message and you have not yet surrendered your life to the Lord Jesus Christ, I would like you to take that decision right there where you are. You must be born again to be a partaker of the blessing of the God of Daniel. Why do not you take that decision today? Right there where you are, the Lord is with you and wants you to come to Him. All you need do is acknowledge the fact that you are a sinner, that you cannot approach God in your sinful state. Repent of your sins right there where you are, confess your sins to Him; name them one by one and ask Him to forgive you and cleanse you from all unrighteousness. Claim the redemptive power in the Blood of Jesus. Renounce the world of sin and the devil. Jesus is waiting for you. Let today be the day when power will change hands in your life and the miracle of God will take root in your life. God will bless you as you take that decision.

Invite the Lord Jesus into your life. Ask Him to come into your heart and become your personal Lord and Saviour. Enthrone Him over your life and ask Him to take control of all that concerns you. Surrender take totality of your life to Him and decide that you will never go back to the world of sin and the devil.

I congratulate you for this decision that you have just taken. It is the most important decision in life. I pray that it shall be permanent in your life in the Name of Jesus. I pray that the Lord will uphold you with His right hand of righteousness and will keep you from falling. I pray that the Lord will write your name in the Book of Life and you will not by any means rub it off in the Name of Jesus. Say bye-bye to the world of darkness and enter into the Kingdom of Light.

The prayers that I am suggesting below are prayers of divine intervention by the God of Daniel. As you pray them, the spirits that have been tormenting you will leave you. The healing power of God will go forth and heal all manner of sicknesses and diseases in your spirit, soul and body. Make sure you do not allow any distraction. Every arrow that has been fired at you will go back to the sender. The power of God will fall upon you and you will be delivered from even terminal diseases. The power of God will pop out like pop-corn and things will begin to happen.

Take these prayer points with holy aggression:
1.   God of Daniel arise and pursue my pursuers in the Name of Jesus.
2.   Every occultic power searching for my face, die in the Name of Jesus.

3. In the presence of those asking for my God, O God of Daniel, manifest your power in the name of Jesus.

4. Every plantation of witchcraft in my body be uprooted in the Name of Jesus

5. I arrest every profitless hard work in the Name of Jesus.

6. I cancel every failure at the edge of breakthroughs in the Name of Jesus.

7. Every ladder of darkness that the enemy has been using to get into my life, break and burn to ashes in the Name of Jesus.

8. Every harassment from the spirit of death and hell cease in the Name of Jesus.

9. Let every mark of hatred upon my forehead; be rubbed off by the Blood of Jesus.

10. God of Daniel, pass through my life with signs and wonders in the Name of Jesus.

11. God of Daniel anoint me for favour in the Name of Jesus.

12. Serpents and Scorpions in my body go back to your sender in the Name of Jesus.

13. Stubborn witchcraft of my father's house, die in the Name of Jesus.

14. Stubborn witchcraft of my mother's house die in the Name of Jesus.

When your star begins to shine, there are some boasting powers that would want to ask questions. These powers would want to impede your movement. Therefore take these prayers with boiling anger.

15. Every child of Belial, every child of Belzebub, I cast you out of my progress in the Name of Jesus.

16. Listen to me, household witchcraft, your time is up; therefore die in the Name of Jesus.

17. Every power that has to die, for my joy to be full die in the Name of Jesus.

18. Doors, Gates of my breakthroughs, open by fire in the Name of Jesus.

19. Every personal wall of Jericho in my life, crumble in the Name of Jesus.

20. I possess my possession in the Name of Jesus.

21. I seal all my prayers with the Blood of Jesus.

▶ CHAPTER 5

Provoke
Your
RAINFALL

To provoke means to deliberately annoy. It means to incite something to do something. It means to incite by arousing anger. It means to stimulate into action. So whenever you say 'provoke,' anger is involved.

When we were very little boys we used to go to play and pluck fruits at a nearby railway compound. One day, somebody took me to the compound and we saw a lot of ripe mangoes and we were throwing stones at them all of a sudden, we heard the barking of a large dog which was rushing towards us with madness. Prior to that time I had never climbed a tree, but when I saw the anger and the violence with which the dog was coming, I found myself on a tree. How I got there I did not know. So something provoked me and I got on top of that tree. You never know what you could do sometimes until you try.

I was a teacher for many years in a secondary school. One day, I was the master on duty and as master on duty you would go round and see that all the students were in the classrooms. One would also go round the toilets and everywhere. As I was going round that day, I noticed the head of a student inside the toilet. When I looked down I did not see the person's legs. I then looked from the top and saw a boy kneeling right on top of the water closet and busy reading a letter. He did not see me for about three minutes. By the time he looked up and saw me, he screamed. I said, "Bring that letter." He said, "No sir, no sir, no sir. Don't read this letter." Any way he gave me the letter with shaking hands. I saw in the first paragraph: "The garden of love, dearest apple of my eye, the sugar in my tea." I said, "What class are you?" He said, "Form 3," that is what we now call JSS III. "Who wrote this letter?" He said, "One girl in form II." I said, "Go and bring the girl." He said, "Ah master, beat me and let me go." I said, "No beating, go and bring the girl." Later he dragged the little girl to me and I said, "You wrote this letter?" She said, "Yes" I said, "Okay, go and bring me your class teacher." She did and the teacher and I looked at the school results to see how well that boy and the girl were doing. I found out that in the last exam the boy was number three to the last person and the girl

DR. D. K. OLUKOYA

was number two to the last. I now said, "Well, if I take you to the Principal you know what will happen." They said, "Yes, he will send us out of this school." I said, "I will not do that. Now you have three weeks to the exams. If your position does not come between number one and number ten, this letter will get to the school authority and both of you will go." They said, "Thank you sir," and went away. Do you know what? What I did to them provoked them into action. They read very hard and they made it.

A sister who was attending my house fellowship, had a dream where some short demons came to confront her. She said, "I bind all of you in the name of Jesus." The demons started to laugh and at the end said, "Everybody is binding and you too you are binding." When she woke up she was mad with anger and went on dry fast and by the time these demons came again she was able to deal with them. That was holy provocation.

The Lord showed me a vision of a cloud of abundance of good rain upon many of God's people. Although the clouds were very dark and

5. When evil powers are challenging God in your life.
6. When you have looked at the whole of your family line and you don't want to follow its evil pattern.
7. When the viper of disgrace that has attached itself to your hand is trying to bite you.
8. When the enemy has sucked you dry.
9. When your debt is mounting and your income is low.
10. When the Lazarus of your destiny has been embalmed and buried.
11. When yokes begin to multiply and chain problems continue to come.
12. When Lodge members, occult people and evil assemblies are saying,
"You better join us."
13. When you are being encouraged to be disobedient to God because you have a problem.
14. When shedding tears have become your regular affair.
15. When the road you are traveling is becoming rougher and rougher.

16. When you notice what we call 'finishing fever' in your life. When spiritual fever starts as you are about to finish something.

17. When you are becoming an expert at finishing what you should not have started.

18. When you try to smile and the smile is not coming at all.

19. When your nose is bleeding and your eyes are black in the boxing ring of life.

HOW DO YOU PROVOKE YOUR RAINFALL?

There is nobody that God does not have a good destiny for. The Bible says, "I know the thoughts that I have towards you, they are the thoughts of good and not of evil." That is what the Bible says, meaning that God does not have terrible or bad destiny for anybody. But the rain of destiny may refuse to fall. How do you speak to the clouds today that they must rain abundance on you? How should you declare that what you have been having are showers of blessing, but now you want the rain to fall? How do you provoke your rainfall?

1. **Disband** worry from your life: John 14:1 says, *"Let not your heart be troubled"* It does not say, "Pray for God not to allow your heart to be troubled." Worry will give you something to do but it won't get you anywhere. It is not your friend at all. It is your enemy. It cannot be found in God's vocabulary. If you read the Bible very well you will find that Jesus was never in a hurry. He knew what He wanted to do and He did it. Anything they said to scare Him did not work. Worry and faith are incompatible, because immediately worry runs in faith jumps out. The beginning of worry is the end of faith. We could see that Elijah was not worried at all. He was confident that that rain would fall.

I remember the story of one little girl. There was no rain in their city and the Christians decided to gather to pray that rain would fall. As they were going for the meeting, the girl said, "Daddy, let me follow you." The daddy said she could come along. Later the girl said, "Daddy, wait I have taken my

Bible but there is something I have forgotten." And she ran inside and took an umbrella. The daddy asked her: "What are you doing with the umbrella?" She said, "Daddy, but we are going to pray that God should send rain." The man laughed and said, "Well, it has not rained for many years." They went and before the prayer meeting got half way rain started. It was only the little girl who had an umbrella.

Worry has nowhere to go and it gets nowhere. Many years ago, when I was in England, one doctor told me a story. He said there was one patient crying every night, "Doctor, give me medicine or I will die. Give me medicine or I will die." The patient was screaming and screaming but they had given him all the medicine that he was to take. When he continued to cry, the doctor went and got water, put it inside the injection and put it on his body then he said thank you and slept. So it was not the sickness that wanted to kill the man, it was worry. Many die before their time because of worry. I remember the day that all the guests in one hotel deserted the hotel. Somebody was crying in one of the rooms: "It is inside my bag." They knocked at the door of that room but the fellow did not open the door. The other guests started running out thinking that the man wanted to bring out a gun from his bag. But the man was just having a dream. He later explained that he found himself inside a house in the dream, the door was locked, he wanted to go out and was looking for his keys and was saying, "It is inside my bag." Worry gets nobody anywhere. That is why Jesus said, *"Be anxious for nothing but in everything by prayer and supplication, let your request be known unto God."* (Philippians 4:6).

When you make your request known unto God, His peace will come.

2. Violent faith: Elijah said to Ahab, "Go, eat and drink for there is the sign of abundance of rain." There was no physical sign of rain but Elijah had evidence of it inside him. I want you by your ears of faith to hear the sound of your breakthroughs today.

3. **Pray until something happens:** Pray until you feel the drops of rain falling on your body. Don't get up until God answers.

4. **Never accept your present position as final:** The enemy might have been playing games with you. Don't agree with his game. Don't negotiate with him at any level. Don't go to his camp to warm yourself in its fire. Because if you warm yourself in his fire you will pay for every heat that you enjoyed there. The devil operates a primitive trade by barter. Everything anybody gets from him, the person will vomit it. So, don't go to him for help. Also, somebody has said that the greatest enemy of success is present achievement: Well, I am doing well; I thank God. So, I don't need to do anything more. Don't accept where you are as your final bus-stop. Don't take your financial position now as your final financial bus-stop. Don't take your spiritual life now as your final spiritual bus-stop.

5. Keep going until you see result: Elijah said, "Go again, go again, go again." Keep going until you see perfection. Don't allow the enemy to make you depressed. All those periods you spend in just sitting down to mourn and in self-sympathy, you allow the enemy to gain on you. If God would open the eyes of some people instead of sitting down to be crying, they will be jumping up and be doing praise worship, because they will see how close they are to what God wants to give them. A lot of us don't understand the principles of God. When you get born again you say, "I want chin-chin and doughnut. He says, 'Take." You say, "That is good. Now, I want goody goody." He says, "Take." Then as you grow in faith you find that sometimes when you ask for something it will be slow in coming. God is training you to see how firm you can stand. Keep going, don't give up. Keep going, keep going. If you pray and after the prayer doubt comes into your mind again, forget that you have prayed, go back again and pray. All the faith preachers who say,

"once you pray once it is okay" are now seeing their mistake. Elijah said, "Go again, go again, go again, go seven times." It was not until the seventh time that some clouds like a little hand came up and then things began to happen.

6.   **Draw near to God:** That is, put away anything offensive to Him in your life. Every apple of the devil has worms in it. If the devil gives you scotch egg to eat, you can be sure that only the flour outside it is good, the egg is bad. If you draw near to God, He too will draw near to you. If you move away from Him, He too will move farther away from you. And since His legs are longer than your own, if He moves back one step He might have moved 500 miles when you have moved only one foot. Draw near to God.

7.   **Pray to provoke a big rain:** Elijah used the weapon of prayer to provoke a big rain. Many people are supposed to be employers

of labour but they are now being employed. Some don't even have a job. They have to provoke rain and by this very tomorrow begin to see it falling upon them.

PRAYER POINTS

1. I provoke my heavens to open, in the name of Jesus. (Pray this seven times and shout seven Hallelujah).
2. Every power that has locked me up, die, in the name of Jesus.
3. My rain of marital, business and career breakthroughs, I provoke you by the blood of Jesus. Fall, in the name of Jesus (Please, be specific).
4. Every power stealing the rain of my blessing, what are you waiting for? Die, in the name of Jesus.
5. Where is the Lord God of Elijah? Provoke my rain of blessing to fall, in the name of Jesus?

YORUBA PUBLICATIONS
1. ADURA AGBAYORI
2. ADURA TI NSI OKE NIDI
3. OJO ADURA

FRENCH PUBLICATIONS
1. PLUIE DE PRIERE
2. ESPIRIT DE VAGABONDAGE
3. EN FINIR AVEC LES FORCES MALEFIQUES DE LA MAISON DE TON PERE
4. QUE l'ENVOUTEMENT PERISSE
5. FRAPPEZ l'ADVERSAIRE ET IL FUIRA
6. COMMENT RECEVIOR LA DELIVRANCE DU MARI ET FEMME DE NUIT
7. CPMMENT SE DELIVRER SOI-MEME
8. POVOIR CONTRE LES TERRORITES SPIRITUEL
9. PRIERE DE PERCEES POUR LES HOMMES D'AFFAIRES
10. PRIER JUSQU'A REMPORTER LA VICTOIRE
11. PRIERES VIOLENTES POUR HUMILIER LES PROBLEMES OPINIATRES
12. PRIERE POUR DETRUIRE LES MALADIES ET INFIRMITES
13. LE COMBAT SPIRITUEL ET LE FOYER
14. BILAN SPIRITUEL PERSONNEL
15. VICTOIRES SUR LES REVES SATANIQUES
16. PRIERES DE COMAT CONTRE 70 ESPIRITS DECHANINES
17. LA DEVIATION SATANIQUE DE LA RACE NOIRE
18. TON COMBAT ET TA STRATEGIE
19. VOTRE FONDEMENT ET VOTRE DESTIN
20. REVOQUER LES DECRETS MALEFIQUES
21. CANTIQUE DES CONTIQUES

22. LE MAUVAIS CRI DES IDOLES
23. QUAND LES CHOSES DEVIENNENT DIFFICILES
24. LES STRATEGIES DE PRIERES POUR LES CELIBATAIRES
25. SE LIBERER DES ALLIANCES MALEFIQUES
26. DEMANTELER LA SORCELLERIE
27. LA DELIVERANCE: LE FLACON DE MEDICAMENT DIEU
28. LA DELIVERANCE DE LA TETE
29. COMMANDER LE MATIN
30. NE GRAND MAIS LIE
31. POUVOIR CONTRE LES DEMOND TROPICAUX
32. LE PROGRAMME DE TRANFERT DE RICHESSE
33. LES ETUDIANTS A l'ECOLE DE LA PEUR
34. L'ETOILE DANS VOTRE CIEL
35. LES SAISONS DE LA VIE
36. FEMME TU ES LIBEREE

ANNUAL 70 DAYS PRAYER AND FASTING PUBLICATIONS

1. Prayers That Bring Miracles
2. Let God Answer By Fire
3. Prayers To Mount With Wings As Eagles
4. Prayers That Bring Explosive Increase
5. Prayers For Open Heavens
6. Prayers To Make You Fulfil Your Divine Destiny
7. Prayers That Make God To Answer And Fight By Fire.

8. Prayers That Bring Unchallengeable Victory And Breakthrough Rainfall Bombardments
9. Prayers That Bring Dominion Prosperity And Uncommon Success
10. Prayers That Bring Power And Overflowing Progress
11. Prayers That Bring Laughter And Enlargement Breakthroughs
12. Prayers That Bring Uncommon Favour And Breakthroughs
13. Prayers That Bring Unprecedented Greatness & Unmatchable Increase
14. Prayers That Bring Awesome Testimonies And Turn Around Breakthroughs.

BOOKS BY PASTOR (MRS) SHADE OLUKOYA

1. Power To Fulfil Your Destiny
2. Principles Of A Successful Marriage
3. The Call of God
4. The Daughters of Phillip
5. When Your Destiny is Under Attack
6. Violence Against Negative Voices
7. Woman of Wonder
8. I Decree An Uncommon Change

The Books, Tapes and CDs (Audio and Video)
All Obtainable At:

☞ Battle Cry Christian Ministries
322, Herbert Macaulay Way, Sabo, Yaba, Lagos
Phone: 0816-122-9775, 0803-304-4239

☞ MFM International Bookshop
13, Olasimbo Street, Onike, Yaba, Lagos

☞ MFM Prayer City
Km 12, Lagos/Ibadan Expressway

☞ 54, Akeju Street, off Shipeolu Street
Palmgrove, Lagos

☞ All MFM Churches Nationwide

☞ All Leading Christian Bookstores

☞ Battle Cry Christian Ministries
Abuja Zonal Office & Bookshop
No 4, Nasarawa Street, Block A, Shop 4, Garki Old Market.
Phone: 0813-499-3860

BOOK ORDER

Is there any book written by
Dr. D. K. Olukoya (General Overseer, MFM Ministries)
that you would like to have:

Have you seen his latest books?
To place an order for this End-Time Materials,

Call: 08161229775

Battle Cry Ministries... equipping the saints of God

God bless.